This book belongs to
_____

This book is dedicated to my children - Mikey, Kobe, and Jojo.

Copyright © 2022 Grow Grit Press LLC. All rights reserved. No part of this book may be reproduced in any form without permission in writing from the publisher. Please send bulk order requests to growgritpress@gmail.com

Paperback ISBN: 978-1-63731-618-4
Hardcover ISBN: 978-1-63731-620-7
eBook ISBN: 978-1-63731-619-1

Printed and bound in the USA.
NinjaLifeHacks.tv

Ninja Life Hacks®
by Mary Nhin

# Ninja Life Hacks®

# CHRISTMAS

A Rhyming Children's Book About Christmas

Ninja Life Hacks®
by Mary Nhin

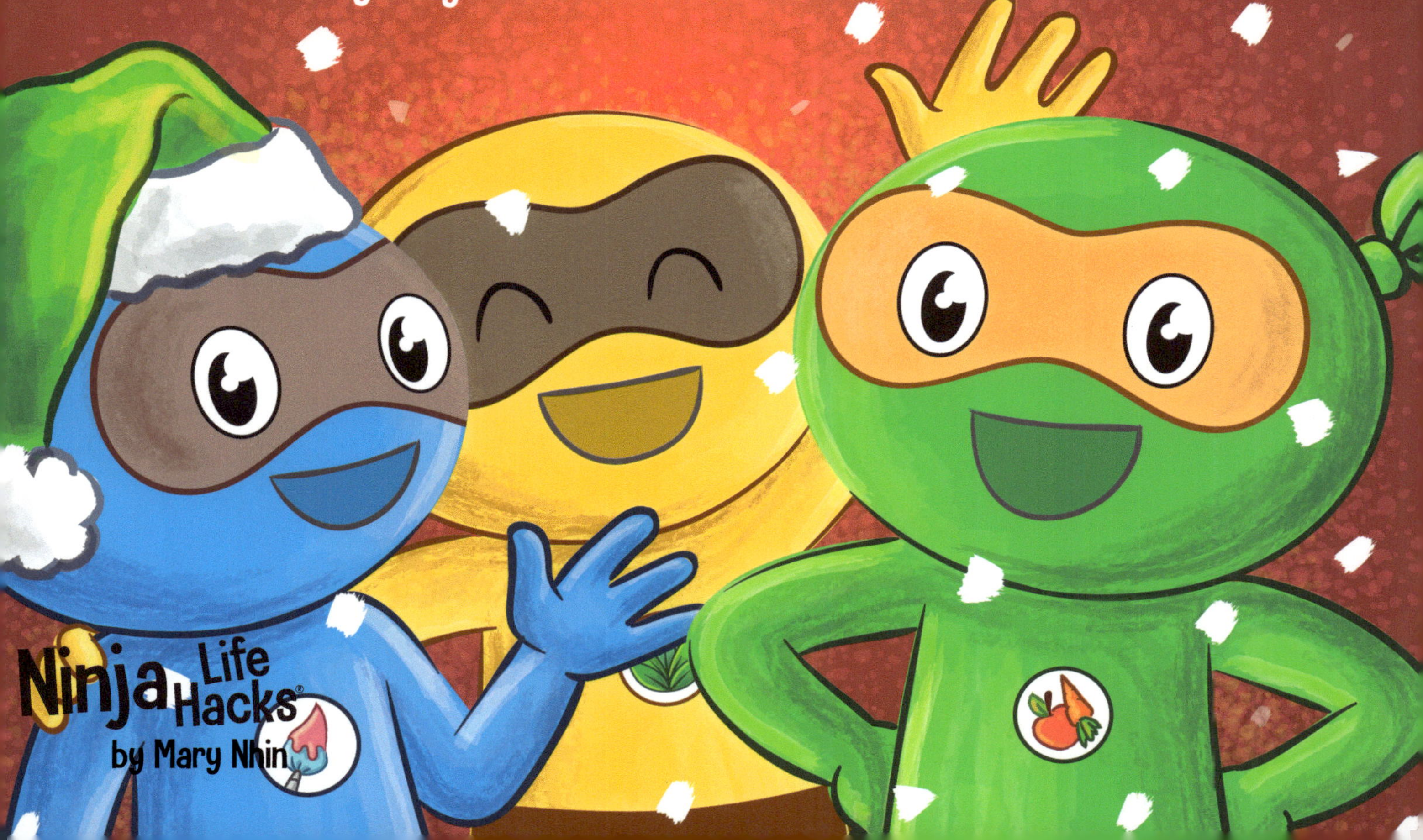

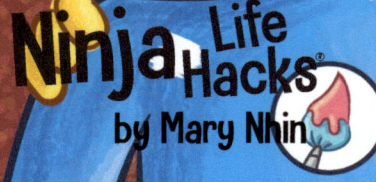

And now will you take a look at that!
The most beautiful tree ever seen!
With so many lights and ornaments,
You can hardly see any green!

Christmas Day dawns bright and clear.
Snow is on every house.
The ninjas race down to see their stockings.
They are **NOT** as quiet as a mouse!

Finally, the gifts are in the right hands.
Everyone's in a good mood.
Except Hangry Ninja, who bangs a knife and fork,
'I need to eat some food!'

Evening sets in, the Ninjas gather around,
Creative Ninja plays a tune.
They all sing Christmas carols at the top of their lungs,
Beneath the light of the moon.

I love to hear from my readers. Email me your feedback or thoughts on what my next story should be at growgritpress@gmail.com

Yours truly, Mary

 @marynhin  @GrowGrit
#NinjaLifeHacks

 Mary Nhin  Ninja Life Hacks

 Ninja Life Hacks

 @ninjalifehacks_tv

www.ingramcontent.com/pod-product-compliance
Lightning Source LLC
Chambersburg PA
CBHW041106070526
44583CB00002B/75